NEW EDITION

Business English

FOR BEGINNERS

WORKBOOK

David Christie

Cornelsen

IMPRESSUM

Business English for Beginners – New Edition Workbook wurde geplant und entwickelt von der Verlagsredaktion der Cornelsen und Oxford University Press GmbH & Co.

Verfasser	David Christie, Banbury
Beraterin	Rita Eibisch, Königs Wusterhausen
Verlagsredaktion	Janan Barksdale
Redaktionelle Mitarbeit	Sylee Gore, Eleanor Toal, Andreas Goebel, Fritz Preuss (Wortliste)
Design & Herstellung	Petra Eberhard, Grafik Design
Bildredaktion	Uta Hübner

Erhältlich sind auch:		
Course book	ISDN-13: 978-3-8109-1982-3;	ISDN-10: 3-8109-1982-9
Audio-CD	ISDN-13: 978-3-8109-1984-7;	ISDN-10: 3-8109-1984-5
Starter pack (Vorkurs mit CD)	ISDN-13: 978-3-8109-1976-2;	ISDN-10: 3-8109-1976-4
Teacher's book	ISDN-13: 978-3-8109-1985-4;	ISDN-10: 3-8109-1985-3

QUELLENVERZEICHNIS

Grafiken: Oxford Designers & Illustrators
Fotos: action press, Hamburg: S. 16/Neumayer, 31/Jossen; **Cal Barksdale:** S. 35, 40; **Bavaria Bildagentur,** München: Titelfoto, 14/Vega; **Carsten L. Bergmann,** Berlin: S. 4 (2), 7, 24 (2); **Jan Chipps Photography,** London: S. 6, 8 (2),14, 16, 52, 57, 58; **COMSTOCK,** Luxemburg: S. 4 (2), 8, 10 (2), 12, 13, 15, 16, 17, 26, 28, 29, 30, 36, 37, 40, 47, 49, 50; **Corbis Stockmarket,** Düsseldorf: S. 19/Steiner, 20/Steiner, 24/Cameron; **Das Fotoarchiv,** Essen: S. 52/Tack; **IFA-Bilderteam,** Düsseldorf: S. 35/Direct Stock; **The IMAGE BANK,** Berlin: S. 5/Klumpp, 22/Mooks, 48/Pistolesi, 53/Coyne/Becker/Nevada Wier, 55/DeLossy; **Picture Press,** Hamburg: S. 27/Lewis, 32

Wir danken folgenden Firmen für die freundliche Unterstützung: Kellogg's, BMW, Fiat

Nicht alle Copyright-Inhaber konnten ermittelt werden; deren Urheberrechte werden hiermit vorsorglich und ausdrücklich anerkannt.

www.cornelsen.de

1. Auflage, 3. Druck 2005

Alle Drucke dieser Auflage können, weil untereinander unverändert, im Unterricht nebeneinander verwendet werden.

© 2002 Cornelsen & Oxford University Press GmbH & Co., Berlin.

Das Werk und seine Teile sind urheberrechtlich geschützt. Jede Nutzung in anderen als den gesetzlich zugelassenen Fällen bedarf der vorherigen schriftlichen Einwilligung des Verlages. Hinweis zu §52a UrhG: Weder das Werk noch seine Teile dürfen ohne eine solche Einwilligung eingescannt und in ein Netzwerk eingestellt werden. Dies gilt auch für Intranets von Schulen und sonstigen Bildungseinrichtungen.

Druck: Druckerei zu Altenburg

ISBN-13: 978-3-8109-1983-0
ISBN-10:   3-8109-1983-7

Inhalt gedruckt auf Recyclingpapier, hergestellt aus 100 % Altpapier.

Vorwort

Dieses Workbook ist eine praktische Unterstützung für die Arbeit mit *Business English for Beginners – New Edition*. Das Englisch, das Sie im Kurs lernen, können Sie im Workbook üben – so bleibt es länger im Gedächtnis. Alle Übungen eignen sich ausgezeichnet als Hausaufgaben zwischen den Unterrichtsstunden.

Wie die Units im Buch, so sind auch die Übungen im Workbook in die Abschnitte A und B unterteilt. Wenn Sie Teil A im Buch abgeschlossen haben, können Sie die A-Übungen im Workbook machen, nach Teil B sind die B-Übungen dran – falls Ihre Kursleiterin bzw. Ihr Kursleiter nicht ein anderes Vorgehen empfiehlt. Am Ende von Abschnitt B finden Sie noch zusätzliche Übungen. Sie unterscheiden sich ein wenig von den vorhergehenden und beinhalten oft auch etwas Neues, z.B. nützliche Ausdrücke oder eine Übung zur Aussprache. Außerdem gibt es drei Tests im Workbook (nach den Units 4, 7 und 10), mit denen Sie Ihre Fortschritte überprüfen können.

Die Lösungen zu den Übungen befinden sich auf den Seiten 60-64. Im Wörterverzeichnis finden Sie alle Wörter und Ausdrücke von A-Z, die nicht (oder zu einem späteren Zeitpunkt) im Kursbuch vorkommen.

Und jetzt viel Erfolg
– und natürlich *Good luck!*

Inhaltsverzeichnis

	UNIT	PAGE
1	You and your job	4
2	In the office	9
3	People and companies	14
4	Daily routines	19
1	TEST	24
5	Doing business	26
6	A visit to a company	30
7	Facts and figures	35
2	TEST	40
8	Trends and sales	42
9	Arrangements	47
10	Travelling on business	52
3	TEST	57
	Lösungen	60
	Wörterverzeichnis	

1 You and your job

Das Verb *to be*: I'm, he's, she's, it's, we're, they're

A.1 Write in the missing parts of the verb *to be*.
Ergänzen Sie die fehlenden Formen des Verbs to be.

Hello. I'm Christa Janssen. I *'m* from Germany. I _____¹ a secretary with a company in Munich.

Hello. I _____² Adam Smith. I _____³ from England. I _____⁴ a manager with a company in London.

Hello. We _____⁵ Carol and Simon. We _____⁶ from the USA. We _____⁷ with a company in Miami, Florida.

A.2 Complete the texts with *he's*, *she's*, *it's* or *they're*.
Vervollständigen Sie die Texte mit he's, she's, it's *oder* they're.

This is Christa Janssen. *She's* from Germany. _____¹ a secretary with a company in Munich.

This is Adam Smith. _____² from England. _____³ a manager with a company in London.

This is Carol and Simon. _____⁴ from the USA. _____⁵ with a company in Miami, Florida.

This is an office. _____⁶ Christa Janssen's office. _____⁷ in Munich.

Fragen stellen mit dem Verb *to be*

FRAGEWORT	*to be*	
Where	are	you from?
What	's (= is)	your name?
Where	's (= is)	he from?
Where	are	they from?
How old	is	she?

BEACHTEN SIE:			
where	+	is	= where's
what	+	is	= what's

A.3 Complete the conversation. *Vervollständigen Sie die Konversation.*

BEN   Hi. My name's Ben.
           _____¹ your name?

JILL   Jill. Where _____²
           _____³ from, Ben?

BEN   I'm from Atlanta, Georgia.
           _____⁴ are you _____⁵ ?

JILL   Oxford, England.

A.4 Answer the questions about Ben. Then write questions for Jill.
Beantworten Sie die Fragen über Ben. Schreiben Sie anschließend Fragen über Jill.

Name	Ben Schuster		Name	Jill Murray
From	Atlanta		From	Oxford
Age	28 years old		Age	30 years old
Job	a sales manager		Job	an accountant
Hobbies	tennis and swimming		Hobbies	jogging and music

1   Where's Ben from?
    He's from Atlanta.

2   How old is he?
    _____

3   What's his job?
    _____

4   What are his hobbies?
    _____

5   *Where's Jill from?*
    She's from Oxford.

6   _____
    She's 30 years old.

7   _____
    She's an accountant.

8   _____
    They're jogging and music.

Die Verneinung von to be: isn't/aren't

A.5 Write in 's, isn't, 're or aren't.
Tragen Sie 's, isn't, 're oder aren't in die Lücken ein.

This is Paul Morris.
1 He ___isn't___ from England.
2 He _____ from the USA.
3 He _____ from Australia.
4 He _____ a travel agent.
5 He _____ 44 years old.
6 He _____ 50 years old.
7 His hobbies _____ music and jogging.
They _____ reading and squash.

```
Name:     Paul Morris
From:     Australia
Age:      44 years old
Job:      a travel agent
Hobbies:  reading and squash
```

Die Possessivpronomen: my/your/his ...

A.6 Write in *my, your, her, its, our* or *their*.
Ergänzen Sie my, your, her, its, our oder their.

1 Hello. _____ name's David. What's _____ name?

2 Jill's hobbies are jogging and music. _____ hobbies are jogging and music.

3 Carol and Simon are from Florida. _____ company is in Miami.

4 Berg is a German company. _____ head office is in Munich.

5 Hello. We're from the USA. _____ names are Carol and Simon.

Writing

A.7 Write 20-30 words about yourself.
Schreiben Sie 20-30 Worte über sich selbst.

- What's your name?
- Where are you from?
- What's your job?
- What are your hobbies?

Am Telefon

B.1 Christa is on the phone. Write in the missing words.
Christa telefoniert gerade. Tragen Sie die fehlenden Wörter ein.

thank | sorry | please | from | speak | spell | moment

CHRISTA   Sales department. Janssen.
WOMAN   Oh, good morning. This is Margaret Wyatt _____¹ London. Can I _____² to Mr Grüneweiler, _____³ ?
CHRISTA   I'm _____⁴ , Mrs … . Can you _____⁵ your name, please?
WOMAN   It's Wyatt. W-Y-A-double T.
CHRISTA   _____⁶ you , Mrs Wyatt. One _____⁷ , please …

EXTRA: Die Welt/Nationalitäten

B.2 Write in the places. *Tragen Sie die Orte ein.*

Australia | Africa | South America | Asia | Japan | Canada

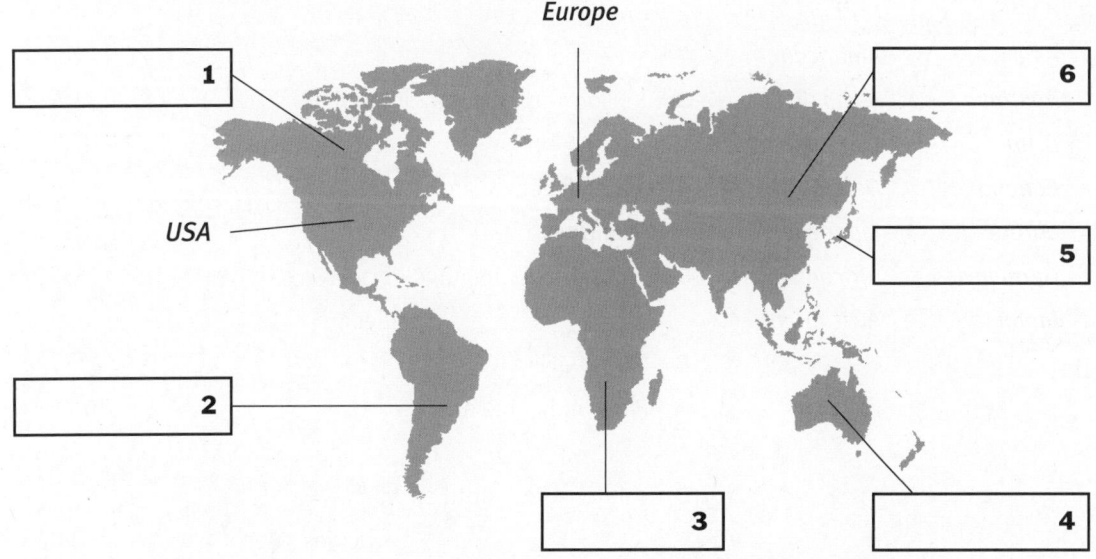

B.3 Where are they from? *Woher kommen sie?*

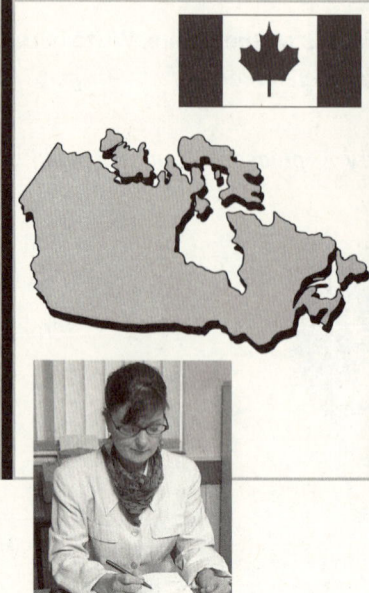

1 This is Mr Tanaka.　　**2** This is Anne.　　**3** This is Lisa and Tim.

He's from Japan. _____　_____

B.4 Match the places to the nationalities. Then complete the sentences.
Ordnen Sie die Nationalitäten den Ortsnamen zu. Vervollständigen Sie dann die Sätze.

Africa	European
America	British
Asia	American
Australia	Asian
Britain	Canadian
Canada	German
Europe	Japanese
Germany	African
Japan	Australian

1 Mr Tanaka is a _Japanese_ businessman.
2 BMW is a _____ car company.
3 Nelson Mandela is a famous _____ politician.
4 India and China are _____ countries.
5 Chicago and Los Angeles are _____ cities.
6 Montreal is a _____ city.
7 Paris and Rome are _____ cities.
8 London and Oxford are _____ cities.

2 In the office

Der Plural von Substantiven

A.1 **Match the numbers to the words.**
Verbinden Sie Ziffern und Zahlwörter.

1	2	3	4	5
6	7	8	9	10
three	nine	two	six	ten
four	one	seven	five	eight

A.2 **Write the number and the plural form of the noun.**
Schreiben Sie die Zahl und das Substantiv im Plural.

1 2 / pen   _two pens_   6   8 / secretary _____
2 4 / lamp   _____   7   5 / diary   _____
3 10 / telephone _____   8   6 / man   _____
4 9 / photo   _____   9   7 / woman   _____
5 3 / fax   _____   10 3 / person   _____

Das Verb *to have got* (haben)

A.3 **Look at the picture, then complete the sentences about Barry's desk.**
Schauen Sie sich die Abbildung an und ergänzen Sie die Sätze über Barrys Schreibtisch.

Barry James is an English businessman.
This is Barry's desk in his office in London.

What has he got on his desk?

1 _He's got a computer._
2 _He's got a_ _____
3 _____
4 _____
5 _____

A.4 Complete what Barry says with *I've got* or *I haven't got*.
Ergänzen Sie Barrys Aussagen mit I've got *oder* I haven't got.

1. __I've got__ a computer.
2. _____ a lamp and a diary.
3. _____ a photo but _____ a plant.
4. _____ a telephone, of course, but _____ a fax machine.

Kurzantworten

A.5 Answer the questions about Jenny.
Beantworten Sie die Fragen über Jenny.

a good job	✓
a nice boss	✓
a car	✗
a hobby	✓
a sister	✗

1. Has she got a good job? __Yes, she has.__
2. Has she got a nice boss? _____
3. Has she got a car? _____
4. Has she got a hobby? _____
5. Has she got a sister? _____

Im Englischen beantworten wir Ja/Nein-Fragen gewöhnlich mit einer **Kurzantwort**, da ein einfaches *Yes* oder *No* oft als unhöflich empfunden wird. Eine Kurzantwort besteht aus Ja bzw. Nein und dem Verb (bzw. Hilfsverb) aus der jeweiligen Frage:
Are you from Germany?
Yes, I am. / No, I'm not.
Have you got a computer?
Yes, I have. No, I haven't.
In Kurzantworten benutzen wir keine Kurzformen von Verben:
Is she a secretary?
Yes, she **is**. ~~Yes, she's.~~
Has she got a car?
Yes, she **has**. ~~Yes, she's.~~

is oder *has*?

A.6 Write the full form *(is or has)*.
*Tragen Sie die vollständige Form (*is* oder* has*) ein.*

1. He's from Germany. → He __is__ from Germany.
2. She's got a new computer. → She _____ got a new computer.
3. What's your name? → What _____ your name?
4. He's got a new car. → He _____ got a new car.
5. It's a BMW. → It _____ a BMW.

there's/there are

A.7 **This is the reception area of a company in England. Are the sentences true or false?** *Auf dem Bild sehen Sie den Empfangsbereich einer Firma in England. Sind die Sätze richtig oder falsch?*

		True	False
1	There are three chairs in the reception area.	☒	☐
2	There's a woman behind the reception desk.	☐	☐
3	There are two magazines on the table.	☐	☐
4	There are two computers on the reception desk.	☐	☐
5	There's a businessman with a newspaper.	☐	☐
6	There's a plant behind the businessman.	☐	☐
7	There are three people near the lift.	☐	☐
8	There's a telephone on the table near the businessman.	☐	☐

A.8 **Rewrite the false sentences from exercise A.7 so that they are true.** *Schreiben Sie die falschen Sätze aus Übung A.7 um, so dass sie richtig sind.*

1   *There's a man ...*
2   _____
3   _____
4   _____

UNIT 2 In the office B

Am Telefon

B.1 Write the telephone numbers.
Schreiben Sie die Telefonnummern in Zahlen.

1. six three five, nine oh one — 635 901
2. seven four seven, double eight four — _____
3. two six five, double oh seven — _____
4. six double six, two double two — _____

B.2 Write the telephone numbers in words.
Schreiben Sie die Telefonnummern in Worten.

1. 711 717 — *seven double one, seven one seven*
2. 459 3062 — _____
3. 458 331 — _____
4. 0044 207 365 221 — _____

B.3 Complete the telephone conversation.
Vervollständigen Sie das Telefongespräch.

| sorry | call | Thank | It's | office | 313 | Can |
| afternoon | from | number | Bye | is | please |

MAN Good afternoon. This _____¹ Steven Harris _____² Johnson & Johnson Ltd. Can I speak to Mrs Westbury, _____³ ?

SECRETARY Good _____⁴ , Mr Harris. I'm _____⁵ , Mrs Westbury isn't in the _____⁶ today. _____⁷ she _____⁸ you back tomorrow morning?

MAN Oh fine. _____⁹ you.

SECRETARY Has she got your _____¹⁰ ?

MAN No. _____¹¹ 01865 749 313.

SECRETARY Sorry. 01865 749 ...

MAN _____¹² .

SECRETARY OK. I've got that.

MAN Thanks. _____¹³ .

SECRETARY Goodbye.

UNIT 2 In the office B | 13

EXTRA: Aussprache

B.4 **How do you say the plural 's'? Put the words in the table and practise saying them.** *Wie spricht man der ‚s' der Pluralform aus? Vervollständigen Sie die Tabelle mit den Wörtern und sprechen Sie sie aus.*

PLURALFORMEN AUSSPRECHEN
[s] (wie in Ne**s**t)
Nach den stimmlosen Lauten f, k, p und t wird das Schluss-'s [s] ausgesprochen:
desk**s**   lamp**s**

[z] (wie in **s**ieben)
Nach stimmhaften Lauten (wie l, m, n, r) und den Vokalen a, i, o und u wird das Schluss-'s [z] ausgesprochen:
pen**s**   telephone**s**   poster**s**   photo**s**

[iz] (wie in b**us**iness)
Nach den Lauten x, ch, sh oder s wird die Endung [iz] ausgesprochen:
fax**es**   offic**es**

desks   bosses
classes
flowers   memos
names
plants   restaurants
telephones

[s] (wie in Ne**s**t)   **[z]** (wie in **s**ieben)   **[iz]** (wie in b**us**iness)
desks

EXTRA: Worträtsel

B.5 **Write in the English words.** *Schreiben Sie die englischen Worte in die Felder.*

1 Schreibtisch
2 drei
3 Kopiergerät
4 neben
5 Ecke
6 Drucker
7 Wand
8 Tür
9 Terminkalender

UNIT 3 People and companies

3 PEOPLE AND COMPANIES

Die einfache Gegenwart: he/she/it

A.1 **Complete the table.** *Vervollständigen Sie die Tabelle.*

INFINITIV	GRUNDFORM	he / she / it + s oder + es
to come (kommen)	come	comes
to go (gehen)	go	
to live (leben)	live	
to speak (sprechen)	speak	
to work (arbeiten)	work	

A.2 **Write in the correct verbs from Exercise A.1.**
Tragen Sie die korrekten Formen aus Übung A.1 ein.

This is John ...

1 He _comes_ from the UK.

2 His hometown is London – he _____ in London.

3 He _____ in an office in London.

4 He _____ English but he _____ to a German class on Fridays.

UNIT 3 People and companies A | 15

A.3 Choose the correct verbs from the list and complete this text about April and her company. *Ergänzen Sie den Text über April und ihre Firma mit den korrekten Formen der angegebenen Verben.*

| to go | to live | to make | to sell |
| to come |

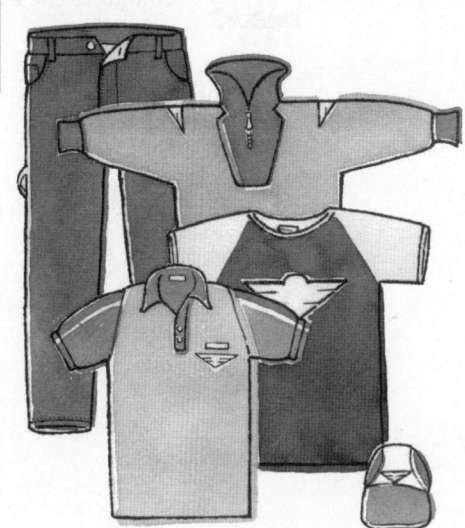

This is April Wilbur. She _comes_ from the USA. Her hometown is Boston, Massachusetts – she _____ ¹ in Boston. April is a marketing manager with a company in Boston. April's company _____ ² clothing (jeans, T-shirts etc). It _____ ³ its products worldwide and April _____ ⁴ to Europe and Japan every year.

Fragen stellen: *does he live? does she go?*

A.4 Complete the questions and answers about John (Exercise A.2). *Vervollständigen Sie die Fragen und Antworten über John.*

1 Where _does_ John come from?
→ He _____ from the UK.
2 Where _____ he _____ ?
→ He lives in London.
3 Where _____ he _____ ?
→ He _____ in an office.
4 Where _____ he _____ on Fridays?
→ He _____ to a German class.

A.5 Answer the questions about April and her company. *Beantworten Sie die Fragen über April und ihre Firma.*

1 Where does April live?
→ _she_ _____
2 What does her company make?
→ _It_ _____
3 Where does it sell its products?
→ _____
4 Where does April go every year?
→ _____

Die einfache Gegenwart: *she lives/she doesn't live*

A.6 Complete the sentences about John and April.
Vervollständigen Sie die Sätze über John und April

1 John comes from the UK, but April __doesn't come__ from the UK. She _____ from the USA.

2 April lives in Boston. John _____ in Boston. He _____ in London.

3 John speaks English. April _____ English, too. But she _____ German.

Reading

A.7 Read the text and answer the questions.
Lesen Sie den Text und beantworten Sie die Fragen.

FedEx (the Federal Express Corporation) is an American transportation company. Every night, it transports five million packages and documents – and it delivers them before 10.30 the next morning. FedEx has got offices worldwide, but its head office is in Memphis, Tennessee. The weather in Memphis is excellent and the company's planes can fly every day.

Cross out the sentence which is not correct.
Streichen Sie die nicht zutreffenden Sätze durch.

1 a ~~FedEx makes planes.~~
  b FedEx transports packages and documents.
2 a Its head office is in Memphis, Tennessee.
  b Its head office is in Chicago, Illinois.
3 a Every night, the company transports 5,000 packages and documents.
  b Every night, the company transports 5 m packages and documents.
4 a FedEx delivers them the next morning.
  b FedEx delivers them the next night.

WORTSCHATZ

transportation	Transport
every night	jede Nacht
to transport	transportieren
package	Paket
to deliver	(aus)liefern
them	sie (Akkusativ)
before	vor
weather	Wetter
excellent	hervorragend
plane	Flugzeug
to fly	fliegen

Leute kennen lernen

B.1 Complete the text.
Vervollständigen Sie den Text.

Hello. My _name's_ Karen West. I'm _____ 1
_____ _____ 2 with
_____ 3 Office Products Ltd in _____ 4 in England.
Our office is in _____ 5 Street.
My telephone number is: oh one two four five
(for Danbury), then _____
_____ 6 and my email
address is karen (small 'k') _____
_____ 7 .

KAREN WEST
Sales Representative

Bell Office Products Ltd
Bell House
20-22 Market Street
DANBURY
CM4 9RR

BELL OFFICE PRODUCTS

Telephone: 01245-201 447
email: karen.west@bell.co.uk

B.2 Underline the best answer.
Unterstreichen Sie die passende Antwort.

1 How do you do.

a Hello.
b I'm fine, thanks.
c How do you do.

4 Where are you from?

a Bremen, in Germany.
b I'm an accountant.
c I'm 28 years old.

2 Please, call me Karen.

a Nice to see you again, too!
b And I'm Hans-Jochen.
c Thank you.

5 What's your phone number?

a It's c.smith@aol.com
b It's 27 Church Street.
c It's 973 4166.

3 How are your children?

a Yes, they are.
b She's fine, thanks.
c They're fine, thanks.

6 Can I introduce Mr Williams?

a How do you do.
b Hi!
c Yes, please.

EXTRA: Who?/-'s

B.3 Look at this company diagram and answer the questions. *Schauen Sie sich das Firmendiagramm an und beantworten Sie die Fragen.*

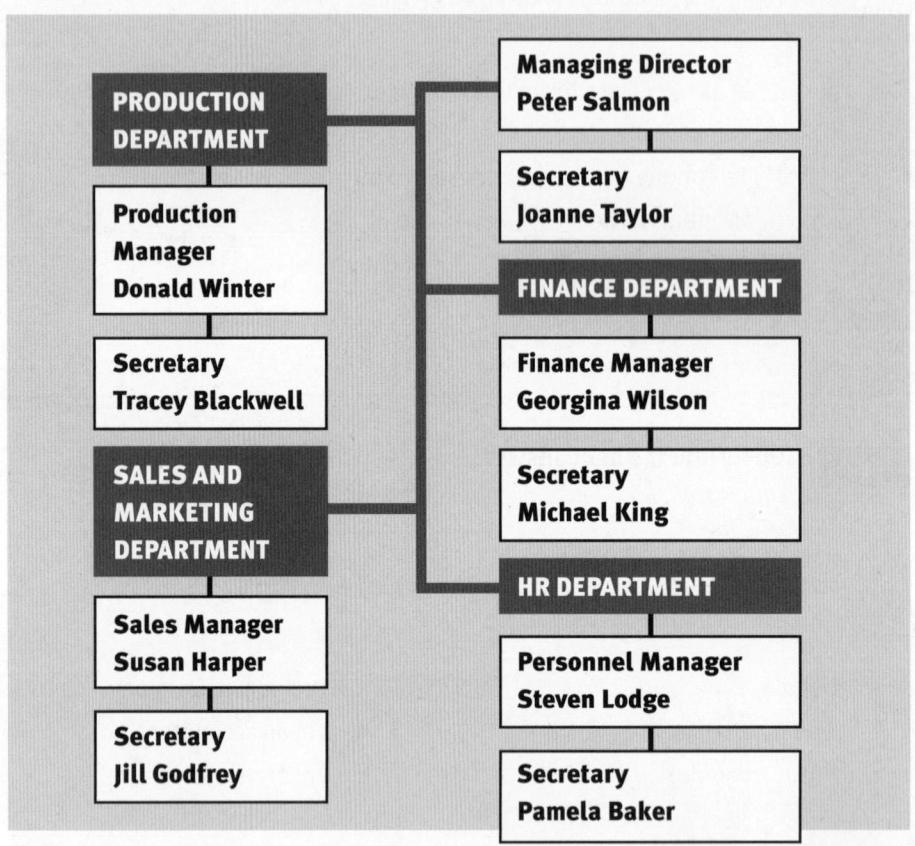

1 Who is the managing director?
   Peter Salmon

2 Who is Peter Salmon's secretary?
   _____

3 Who is the sales manager?
   _____

4 Who is Steven Lodge's secretary?
   _____

5 Who is Jill Godfrey's boss?
   _____

6 Who is Tracey Blackwell's boss?
   _____

B.4 Complete the sentences. *Ergänzen Sie die Sätze.*

1 Georgina Wilson's __secretary__ is Michael King.

2 Susan _____ secretary is Jill Godfrey.

3 Pamela _____ boss is the personnel manager.

4 The production _____ secretary is Tracey Blackwell.

4 Daily routines

Die einfache Gegenwart: *she works/I work*

A.1 Read about Claire. Then complete her sentences.

Claire Wilkins works for an insurance company in England.
She lives in Colchester, about 50 miles (80 kilometres) from London.
She's a personnel officer.

This is a typical day for Claire …

> She goes to work by car.

> She starts work at half past eight.

> She has lunch at about one o'clock. She normally eats in the company canteen.

> She finishes work at half past five. Then she goes home.

Hello. My name's Claire Wilkins. I work for an insurance company near London. I __go__ to work by car. I _____¹ work at half past eight. I _____² lunch at about one o'clock. I normally _____³ in the company canteen. I _____⁴ work at half past five. Then I _____⁵ home.

A.2 Complete the table.

	TO WORK	TO GO	TO HAVE
I	*work*	_____	_____
he/she/it	_____	*goes*	_____
we / you / they	_____	_____	*have*

Fragen stellen: *does she ... ? / do you ... ?*

A.3 Complete the questions with *does* or *do*.

1 How ___does___ Claire go to work?
2 When _____ she start work?
3 Where _____ she have lunch?
4 When _____ she finish work?

5 How _____ you go to work, Claire?
6 When _____ you start work?
7 Where _____ you have lunch?
8 When _____ you finish work?

Die einfache Gegenwart: *she doesn't / they don't ...*

A.4 Complete the text with *doesn't* or *don't*.

Claire and Janet work together in their company's personnel department. Janet _____¹ live in Colchester, she lives in London. She _____² come to work by car, she comes by train.

Claire and Janet _____³ have a big office, but it's very nice. They _____⁴ have a photocopier, but there's a printer and a fax machine.

Claire usually goes to the canteen at one o'clock but Janet _____⁵ usually have lunch. But on Friday, they sometimes go to a café near the office.

sometimes, often, always ...

A.5 Write sentences.

1 I/at/start/usually/work/8 o'clock
   I usually start work at 8 o'clock.

2 I/by/work/go/to/normally/car
   _____

3 I/in/the/have/lunch/canteen/often
   _____

4 café/go/sometimes/I/to/a
   _____

5 I'm/busy/always
   _____

6 never/I'm/late
   _____

BEACHTEN SIE:

Ausdrücke wie *sometimes /often / always /usually / normally /never* stehen **nach** *to be*, aber **vor** anderen Verben:

I'm **normally** at home in the evening.

I **always** start work at 7 o'clock.

What's the time? It's ...

A.6 Write the times in words.

one o'clock   *five to seven*   *five past nine*   _____ 1

_____ 2   _____ 3   _____ 4   _____ 5

_____ 6   _____ 7   _____ 8   _____ 9 oder _____ 10

Freizeitaktivitäten

B.1 Look at the statistics. Then complete the sentences.

FREE TIME IN THE USA
What do Americans like doing in their free time?

KEEPING FIT	76%
GOING TO MOVIES	66%
GOING TO THEME PARKS (eg Disneyland)	57%
PLAYING A SPORT	45%
WATCHING A LIVE SPORT (eg baseball)	43%
COMPUTER HOBBIES	40%

A 'ballgame'. 43% of Americans like watching a live sport.

1 43% of Americans like _____.

2 _____ % of Americans like playing a sport.

3 57% like _____.

4 40% _____ computer hobbies.

5 _____ like going to movies, but the 'top' activity is _____. That's a free-time activity for 76% of Americans.

B.2 Answer the questions for yourself with *Yes, I do/No, I don't/Yes, sometimes.*

1 Do you like keeping fit?

2 Do you like going to movies?

3 Do you play football, hockey or tennis?

4 Do you watch television in the evening?

5 Do you like eating with friends?

6 Do you like cooking?

7 Do you like reading?

8 Do you like learning English?

EXTRA: Aussprache

B.3 Look where the stress *(Betonung)* is in these words and write them in the correct column. Then say the sentences.

morning	popular	colleagues	concerts
company	family	canteen	jogging
address		minutes	

A ●●	B ●●	C ●●●
morning		

> Good morning!

> Jogging is popular with my colleagues.

> What's your address?

> Do you like going to concerts?

> Has your company got a canteen?

> It's ten minutes past ten.

Writing

B.4 Complete the text for yourself.

My Day

"Hello. My name's _____ . I live in _____, in _____ (Germany? Austria? … ?). I usually have breakfast in the morning at _____ . I normally have _____ (muesli? toast? corn flakes? bread? eggs? coffee? tea? milk?). I have lunch at _____ . / (I don't have lunch!) In the evening, I often/usually/sometimes _____ _____.

In my free time, I like _____ _____."

Test 1

Check your English on units 1–4! *Kreuzen Sie die richtigen Antworten an. (Es gibt jeweils nur eine richtige Antwort.)*

David Green
Berg UK Ltd
London

Ilko Martinovich
Expo Vienna

Christa Janssen
Berg GmbH   Munich

Grammatik

1 Christa ... a secretary.

a am ☐
b are ☐
c is ☐
d she's ☐

2 David ... accountant.

a is a ☐
b is an ☐
c are a ☐
d are an ☐

3 Christa's hobbies are jogging and skiing. ... hobbies are jogging and skiing.

a their ☐
b his ☐
c our ☐
d her ☐

4 ... hobbies are tennis and squash.

a David ☐
b David's ☐

5 Berg is an international company. ... sales offices in England, the USA, Australia and Japan.

a It is got ☐
b It have got ☐
c It has got ☐
d She has got ☐

6 ... a factory in Korea, too.

a There's ☐
b There are ☐

7 Ilko Martinovic ... in Germany.

a don't live ☐
b doesn't live ☐

8 He ... in Vienna, in Austria.

a lives ☐
b live ☐

9 Christa and David ... in Austria.
- a don't live ☐
- b doesn't live ☐

10 They ... in Germany and England.
- a lives ☐
- b live ☐

11 Ilko ... to trade fairs.
- a often goes ☐
- b goes often ☐

12 Does Ilko work in his office, too?
- a Yes, he is. ☐
- b Yes, he do. ☐
- c Yes, he doesn't. ☐
- d Yes, he does. ☐

Wortschatz

13 My company ... *(verkauft)* electronic products.
- a sells ☐
- b makes ☐
- c does ☐
- d manufactures ☐

14 I usually have ... at midday.
- a breakfast ☐
- b lunch ☐
- c dinner ☐

15 What ... *(Abteilung)* does she work in?
- a department ☐
- b head office ☐
- c sales ☐

16 In my free time I like ... to music.
- a watching ☐
- b reading ☐
- c listening ☐

Situationen

17 - Can you ... your name please?
     - Yes. S-C-H-M-I-D-T.
- a speak ☐
- b spell ☐
- c write ☐

18 Can he ... ? *(Sie zurückrufen)*
- a call you back ☐
- b you call back ☐
- c call back you ☐

19 She's in a meeting ... the moment.
- a in ☐
- b at ☐
- c with ☐

20 Can I ... Jackie? *(vorstellen)*
- a meet ☐
- b excuse ☐
- c introduce ☐

Total   /20

5 Doing business

Wochentage

A.1 Complete the puzzle.

1. The day before Friday
2. Two days before Wednesday
3. The day after Friday
4. Two days after Sunday
5. Four days before Tuesday
6. The day after Saturday
7. The day before Thursday

was/had

A.2 Read about Mr Pozinski. Then write *was* or *had* in the sentences.

Scott Pozinski is a busy man. He's the US sales manager for Megasoft, a large American software company.

This was Mr Pozinski's diary last week.

MONDAY
Meeting with Laura Giuliani 10.30.

TUESDAY
Trade Fair in Houston.

WEDNESDAY
Lunch with Brad Major 1.00.

THURSDAY
Conference in Miami.

FRIDAY
Interview, CNN studio 11.45

SATURDAY/SUNDAY

1. On Monday Mr Pozinski _had_ a meeting with Laura Giuliani.
2. On Tuesday he _____ at a trade fair in Houston, Texas.
3. He _____ lunch with Brad Major on Wednesday.
4. On Thursday he _____ at a conference in Miami, Florida.
5. At 11.45 on Friday morning he _____ in the CNN studio for a television interview.

was/were

A.3 Complete the table and the sentences with *was* or *were*.

I	_____
he / she / it	_____
we / you / they	_____

1 Where __*were*__ you on Monday?
  I __*was*__ in London.
2 Where _____ Mr Pozinski on Tuesday?
  He _____ in Houston, Texas.
3 Where _____ we on Wednesday?
  We _____ in our office.

Monate/Datumsangaben

A.4 Tick (✓) the correct answer.

SPECIAL DAYS IN THE USA

1 **Independence Day** in the USA is on:
   ☐ a the fourth of June
   ☐ b the fourth of July
   ☐ c the fourteenth of July

Independence Day in the USA

2 **Thanksgiving** is in:
   ☐ a September
   ☐ b October
   ☐ c November

3 **Groundhog Day** is when Americans hope that it's the end of winter. It's on:
   ☐ a the second of January
   ☐ b the second of February
   ☐ c the second of March

A.5 Write the dates in words. Then practise saying them.

1 4 July
   the fourth of July

2 1 April
   _____

3 2 March
   _____

4 3 January
   _____

5 10 September
   _____

6 30 December
   _____

7 21 June
   _____

8 29 October
   _____

Reading

B.1 Read the article and answer the questions.

'From Mouse to House'

SARAH MACMILLAN is a busy secretary and the mother of two small children.

For Sarah, shopping at the supermarket was always a problem. Now she doesn't go to her supermarket, it comes to Sarah.

Like a lot of supermarkets in the UK, her supermarket is now online. Every Thursday evening, Sarah visits its website.

She has her shopping list and clicks on pictures of the supermarket's products. She pays online with her credit card.

Sarah finishes work at half past three on Fridays ... and at 4 o'clock the supermarket delivers her food. Easy. 'From mouse to house'.

WORTSCHATZ

mother	*Mutter*
shopping	*Einkaufen*
supermarket	*Supermarkt*
like	*wie*
credit card	*Kreditkarte*
to deliver	*ausliefern*
food	*Lebensmittel*
easy	*einfach*

1 What does Sarah MacMillan do? _____

2 What was always a problem for Sarah? _____

3 When does Sarah visit her supermarket's website? _____

4 How does she pay? _____

5 When does the supermarket deliver her food? _____

EXTRA: Aussprache und Rechtschreibung

B.2 Say the sentences.

- How do you do.
- Where do you work?
- There were four people in the meeting.
- Her boss isn't here today.
- Our old office was near London.

Now cross out the word that sounds different *(anders klingt)*.

1	~~how~~	do	you
2	were	her	where
3	there	here	near
4	to	no	two
5	do	you	go
6	four	our	for

B.3 There is one spelling mistake in each sentence. Correct the word that is wrong.

1 There are <u>eigth</u> people in my office.   *eight*
2 Were are you from?
3 What's your email adress?
4 Can you spell your name, plese?
5 There office is in Market Street.

6 A visit to a company

Einfache Vergangenheit

A.1 Write in the simple past of these regular verbs.
Then complete the table below.

This is Jane Barclay. She's an international sales manager with a company in England. Her firm's head office is in London.

In her job, Jane often visits companies abroad …

Simple present	Simple past
1 Jane often visits companies abroad.	Last week she ___visited___ Berne.
2 She often travels by plane.	She _____ by plane last week.
3 She often stays at a hotel.	She _____ at a hotel in Berne.
4 She often talks about her company's products and discusses prices.	She _____ about her company's products and _____ prices with the client in Berne.

The simple past (regular verbs)

	to visit	to travel	to arrive
I	visited	_____	_____
he / she / it	_____	_____	_____
we / you / they	_____	_____	_____

BEACHTEN SIE

Bei den meisten Verben wird einfach *-ed* angehängt.
Bei *to travel* wird das *l* verdoppelt.
Bei Verben, die auf *-e* enden, wird nur *-d* angefügt.

A.2 Write in the simple past of these irregular verbs.

1 to fly   _flew_
2 to go   _____
3 to have _____
4 to take _____

Auch unregelmäßige Verben bilden in der Vergangenheit nur eine Form für alle Personen (I, you, he, she, we ...), enden jedoch nicht auf -ed. Auf Seite 99 des Course book finden Sie eine Liste unregelmäßiger Verben.

I	
he, she, it	**flew**
we, you, they	

A.3 Complete the text with the simple past of the verbs in brackets [...].

Last week Jane _visited_ [visit] a client in Berne, Switzerland.

She _____ ¹ [travel] to Berne by plane. She _____ ² [fly] from Heathrow Airport in London on Monday morning and _____ ³ [arrive] at midday. She _____ ⁴ [take] a taxi from the airport to her hotel.

Jane _____ ⁵ [stay] in the hotel on Monday night, then on Tuesday morning she _____ ⁶ [go] to her client's office. They _____ ⁷ [talk] about her company's products and _____ ⁸ [discuss] prices, then they _____ ⁹ [have] lunch. In the afternoon, Jane _____ ¹⁰ [go] back to the airport and _____ ¹¹ [return] to London.

Fragen und Verneinungen: did/didn't

Im **simple present** bilden wir Fragen und verneinte Sätze mit *do* und *don't* für *I, you, we* und *they*, und mit *does* und *doesn't* für *he, she* und *it*: 'Where do you live?' 'He doesn't live in London'.
Im **simple past** benutzen wir *did* und *didn't* für alle Personen (*I, you, he, she, it, we, they*) und sowohl bei regelmäßigen als auch bei unregelmäßigen Verben.

A.4 Complete the questions about Jane.

1 What city *did* Jane *visit* last week? She **visited** Berne in Switzerland.
2 How _____ she _____? She **travelled** by plane.
3 When _____ she _____? She **flew** on Monday morning.
4 When _____ she _____? She **arrived** at midday.
5 How _____ she _____ to the airport? She **went** by taxi.
6 Where _____ she _____? She **stayed** at a hotel.
7 When _____ she _____ to her client's office? She **went** to her client's office on Tuesday morning.
8 What _____ they _____ about? They **talked** about products.
9 Where _____ they _____ lunch? They **had** lunch in a restaurant.
10 When _____ Jane _____ to London? She **returned** to London on Tuesday afternoon.

A.5 Write the negative sentences.

The British millionaire Sir Richard Branson also flew from London to Berne last week.

1 Sir Richard flew first class.
   Jane didn't fly first class!

2 Sir Richard went to his hotel by limousine.
   Jane didn't _____

3 Sir Richard stayed at the Schweizerhof Hotel.
   _____

4 He had lunch with Steven Spielberg.
   _____

Betreuung eines Gastes

B.1 Jane is at her client's office in Berne. She's with her client's PA, Helga. Complete their conversation.

> could I | along the corridor | PA | a coffee | Would you like
> flight | meet

HELGA Jane? Hi, good morning. I'm Helga, Mr Antl's _____ 1.

JANE Hello, Helga. Nice to _____ 2 you.

HELGA How was your _____ 3 ?

JANE Fine, thanks.

HELGA Great. OK. _____ 4 to come this way? ...
Here we are. Would you like _____ 5 ?

JANE No, I'm fine thanks. But _____ 6 use your toilet, please?

HELGA Sure. It's just _____ 7.

EXTRA (1): Aussprache

B.2 Say the words. Then read the sentences.

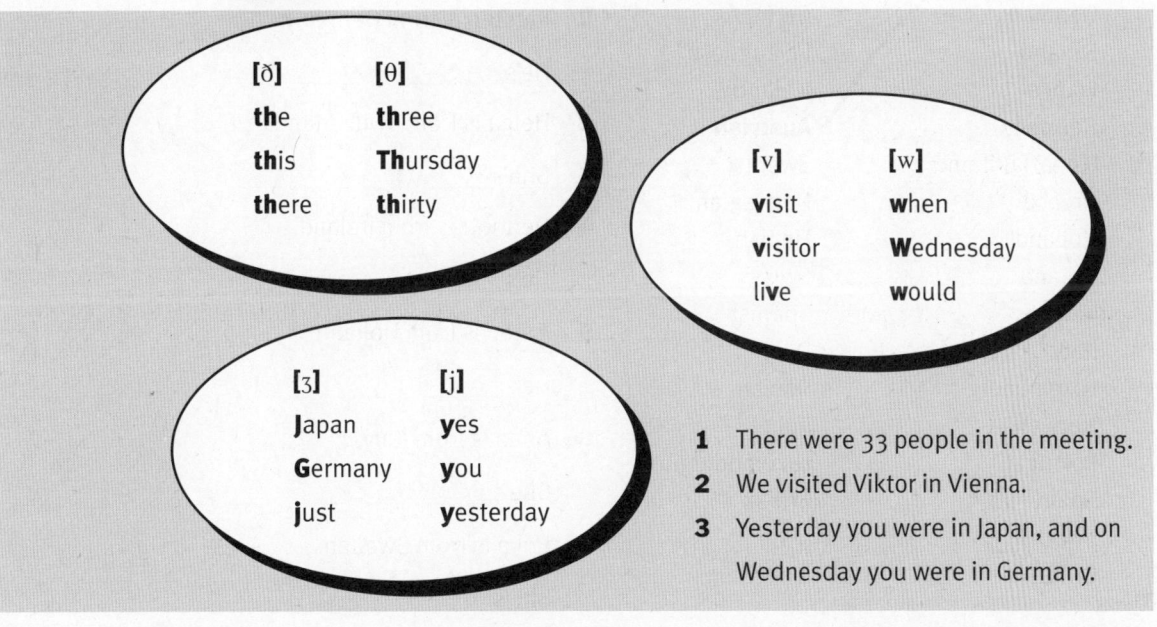

[ð] [θ]
the **th**ree
this **Th**ursday
there **th**irty

[v] [w]
visit **w**hen
visitor **W**ednesday
li**v**e **w**ould

[ʒ] [j]
Japan **y**es
Germany **y**ou
just **y**esterday

1 There were 33 people in the meeting.
2 We visited Viktor in Vienna.
3 Yesterday you were in Japan, and on Wednesday you were in Germany.

EXTRA (2): *Europe*

B.3 Write the country.

1. Oslo is in *Norway.*
2. Paris is in ___
3. Berne is in ___
4. Athens is in ___
5. Madrid is in ___
6. Amsterdam is in ___
7. Reykjavik is in ___

B.4 Match the countries to the nationalities, then complete the sentences.

Austria	Belgian
Belgium	Greek
Denmark	German
Finland	Portuguese
France	Icelandic
Germany	**Austrian**
(Great) Britain	Swedish
Greece	Norwegian
Holland	Finnish
Iceland	Swiss
Ireland	Spanish
Italy	Dutch
Luxembourg	Danish
Norway	Italian
Portugal	Luxembourgian
Spain	British
Sweden	Irish
Switzerland	French

1. Jean-Pierre is from France.
   He's *French.*
2. Karsten is from Germany.
   He's ___
3. Helga is from Switzerland.
   She's ___
4. Dermott is from Ireland.
   He's ___
5. Anton is from Holland.
   He's ___
6. Anna is from Italy.
   She's ___
7. Erika is from Sweden.
   She's ___

7 Facts and figures

Firmenbeschreibung

A.1 Write in the words.

> president | employees | shops
> sells | worldwide | company
> customers | based | profit | began

Coffee 'n' Donuts is an American _____ 1. It _____ 2 in 1953 and it _____ 3 (of course) coffee and doughnuts. There are now two thousand Coffee 'n' Donuts coffee _____ 4 in the States. The company's typical _____ _____ 5 are people like Chuck, Meg and Lauren: young and busy.

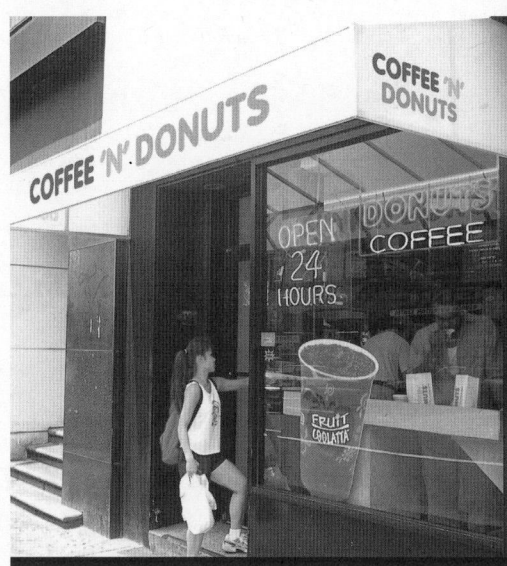

The company is _____ 6 in Chicago, Illinois and its _____ 7 is Benton T. Schutz. Six thousand people work for the company in the USA, and _____ 8 it has 120,000 _____ 9. Coffee 'n' Donuts made a _____ 10 last year of $250m.

A.2 Match the expressions which have the same meaning.

1 the company is based in   the company was established
2 the company began   the company has 1,000 employees
3 the company makes   the company's head office is in
4 1,000 people work for the company   the company manufactures

UNIT 7 Facts and figures A

How much?/How many?

A.3 Underline the countable words in the box. Complete the questions with *How much* or *How many*, then write the answers.

> **(a) pizza** | coffee | (an) egg | soda (e.g. cola) | ice cream
> cheese | (a) hamburger | popcorn

1 _How many_ pizzas does the average American eat each year? 46
2 _____ coffee does he/she drink? _____
3 _____ soda does he/she drink? _____
4 _____ hamburgers does he/she eat? _____
5 _____ ice cream does he/she eat? _____
6 _____ eggs? _____
7 _____ cheese? _____
8 _____ popcorn? _____

What do Americans eat and drink?

Every year, the average American eats:

- 150 hamburgers (3 each week)
- 46 pizzas
- 15 gallons of popcorn (about 68 litres)
- 24 pounds (about 12 kilos) of ice cream
- 28 pounds of cheese
- 243 eggs (eggs and egg products eg pancakes)

and drinks:

- 26 gallons of coffee (about 120 litres)
- 47 gallons of soda – eg cola (over 4 litres every week)

UNIT **7** Facts and figures **A** | 37

much/many/a lot of

A.4 Complete the text with *much*, *many* or *a lot of*.

What is a typical customer?

Jamie Lee Hunt is the manager of a *Coffee 'n' Donuts* in Boston, Massachusetts.

Boston is a beautiful city and in the summer we have __a lot of__ tourists in our coffee shop. There are _____¹ offices near here, too, and _____² our customers are business people. Often, they don't have _____³ time. _____⁴ businessmen and women telephone our shop and we deliver coffee and donuts to their desks. We don't have _____⁵ business customers at night, of course, but then there are _____⁶ taxi drivers in here. And people say that Coffee 'n' Donuts shops are very safe at night – there are always _____⁷ cops near a Coffee 'n' Donuts!

How much is it?

A.5 Write and say the prices in words.

Great Britain
£1	one pound
50p	fifty pence/50p ('p')
£1.99	one pound ninety-nine
£4.20	four pound**s** twenty

USA
$1	one/a dollar
50¢	fifty cents
$1.99	one/a dollar ninety-nine
$4.20	four dollar**s** and twenty cent**s**

Euros
€1	one euro
€1.50	one euro fifty/one euro and fifty cent**s**
€5.35	five euro**s** thirty-five/five euro**s** and thirty-five cent**s**

1 10p — *ten pence (or ten 'p')*
2 £1.50 _____
3 £7.50 _____
4 £2.99 _____
5 10¢ — *ten cents*
6 $1.50 _____
7 $6.50 _____
8 $23.99 _____
9 €1 — *one euro*
10 €3.50 _____
11 €10.65 _____
12 €0.50 _____

Reading

B.1 Read the text and answer the questions.

The Story of Kellogg's®

About 120 years ago, Dr John Harvey Kellogg was a doctor at a clinic in Battle Creek, Michigan. Dr Kellogg invented a new breakfast for his patients: 'corn flakes'. He made the corn flakes from maize ('corn' in America).

Dr Kellogg's patients (and a lot of other people) loved the new corn flakes. Dr Kellogg's brother, William Keith, was a clever businessman, and he saw a business idea. In 1906, the two brothers opened a small factory in Battle Creek and began the *Battle Creek Toasted Corn Flake Company*.

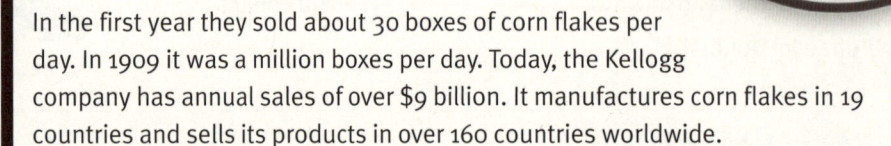

In the first year they sold about 30 boxes of corn flakes per day. In 1909 it was a million boxes per day. Today, the Kellogg company has annual sales of over $9 billion. It manufactures corn flakes in 19 countries and sells its products in over 160 countries worldwide.

1. What did Dr John Harvey Kellogg invent?

2. Who saw 'a business idea'?

3. When did the brothers open their factory?

4. How many boxes of corn flakes did they sell per day in 1909?

5. In how many countries does Kellogg's sell its products today?

VOCABULARY

clinic	*Klinik*
to invent	*erfinden*
patient	*Patient/in*
maize (BE)	*Mais*
corn (AE)	*Mais*
to love	*lieben*
clever	*schlau, klug*
saw	*sah*
idea	*Idee*
box	*Packung*
annual sales	*Jahresumsatz*
over	*über, mehr als*

UNIT 7 Facts and figures B | 39

EXTRA (1): Aussprache

B.2 Write the words in the correct columns. Then say the sentences.

August | conference | discuss | document | Japan | moment
normally | president | product | secretary | student | telephone | total

A ●●	B ●●	C ●●●
August		

- My holiday is in August.
- We sell our products in Japan.
- The president is at a conference.
- One moment, please.
- What's your telephone number?

- We've got a total of 200 students.
- I'm her secretary.
- Can we discuss this?
- Have you got that document?
- I normally have lunch at two.

EXTRA (2): Worträtsel

B.3 Write in the simple past of the irregular verbs.

1 fly
2 begin
3 take
4 meet
5 have
6 do
7 send

4 make
8 go
9 get
10 sell
11 eat

Test 2

Check your English on units 5-7! *Kreuzen Sie die richtigen Antworten an. (Es gibt jeweils nur eine richtige Antwort.)*

Grammatik

1 ... people like coffee.

a A lot of ☐
b Many ☐
c Much ☐

2 – How ... is a muffin?
– $1.50.

a much ☐
b many ☐
c costs ☐

3 Sorry, I don't have ... time.

a much ☐
b many ☐

4 How ... people live here?

a much ☐
b many ☐

5 Ilko often visits other countries.
Last week, he ... Spain.

a visits ☐
b visit ☐
c visited ☐

6 – Where ... ?
– He stayed in a hotel.

a stayed he ☐
b did he stayed ☐
c did he stay ☐

7 – Did he travel by car?
– No, he ... by car.
He travelled by plane.

a didn't travel ☐
b didn't travelled ☐
c doesn't travelled ☐

8 He ... .

a flew ☐
b flyed ☐
c flewed ☐

Wortschatz

9 – What's the ... today?
– It's the 5th of June.

a day ☐
b date ☐
c month ☐

10 The meeting was ... Monday.
- a in
- b at
- c on

11 At 10 o'clock ... the morning.
- a in
- b at
- c on

12 You can visit Expo's ... at www.expo.at.
- a online
- b web page
- c website
- d address

13 *Coffee 'n' Donuts* is ... company.
- a a american
- b an american
- c a American
- d an American

14 It has 120,000 ... *(Angestellte)* worldwide.
- a employees
- b business partners
- c managers

15 It made a ... of $750m.
- a money
- b price
- c profit

Situationen

16 Hello. Nice to ... you!
- a meet
- b meeting

17 How was your ... ?
- a flight
- b airport
- c fly

18 ... to come this way?
- a Do you like
- b Would you like
- c Could you like

19 ... your phone please?
- a May I take
- b Would I use
- c Could I use

20 Yes, ...
- a please
- b thanks
- c certainly

Total /20

8 Trends and sales

Verlaufsform der Gegenwart: *to be + verb + -ing*

A.1 Find the beginnings of the sentences in Box A and write them in Box B.

This is Lester Young. Lester is always busy. Very busy! It's six o'clock in the morning and Lester is at the airport. What is he doing?

A
He's reading
He's writing
He's drinking
He's eating
He's making
~~He's sitting~~

B
1 _He's sitting_ at the airport.
2 _____ coffee.
3 _____ a phone call.
4 _____ a newspaper.
5 _____ a sandwich.
6 _____ an email.

Die *-ing*-Form

A.2 Write the *-ing* forms.

1 do — _doing_
2 send — _____
3 work — _____
4 speak — _____
5 smoke — _____
6 wear — _____
7 say — _____
8 go — _____
9 come — _____
10 jog — _____

DIE -ING-FORM
Bei den meisten Verben wird einfach *-ing* an die Grundform angehängt:
drink drink**ing**

Bei Verben, die auf *-e* enden, fällt das 'e' weg:
writ**e** writ**ing**

Einsilbigen Verben, die auf Vokal + Konsonant (außer 'y') enden, verdoppeln den Konsonanten:
si**t** si**tt**ing
pla**y** pla**ying**

UNIT **8** Trends and sales **A** | 43

Fragen: *Are you ... -ing?*

A.3 Write the questions and answers.

Hello. I'm Helen. I'm sitting in the park at the moment. I'm eating an apple and reading a book. The weather is nice today, and I'm wearing jeans and a T-shirt.

1 is/where/Helen/sitting
   Q *Where is Helen sitting?*
   A *She's sitting in the park.*

2 eating/Helen/is/what
   Q _____
   A _____

3 is/what/reading/she
   Q _____
   A _____

4 what/she/is/wearing
   Q _____
   A _____

BEACHTEN SIE:
Das *present continuous* verwenden wir für **Handlungen**, also Dinge, die man **tun** kann. Es wird nicht bei Verben wie *to be* oder *to have got* benutzt.

A.4 What are these people doing in the park? Complete the questions and write an answer.

1   2   3

What *is* Rebecca doing?

What _____ Kevin and Roy doing?

_____ Ann, Lisa and Caroline _____?

She's jogging.

_____   _____

UNIT 8 Trends and sales A

Einfache Gegenwart/Verlaufsform der Gegenwart

A.5 Write the sentences.

Helen works in a bank. She's the bank manager's assistant. At work, she writes letters, sends emails and makes phone calls every day. She wears smart clothes at work, too. She usually wears a skirt and a jacket. Helen works every week from Monday to midday on Saturday.

But today is Sunday.
Helen isn't working today.

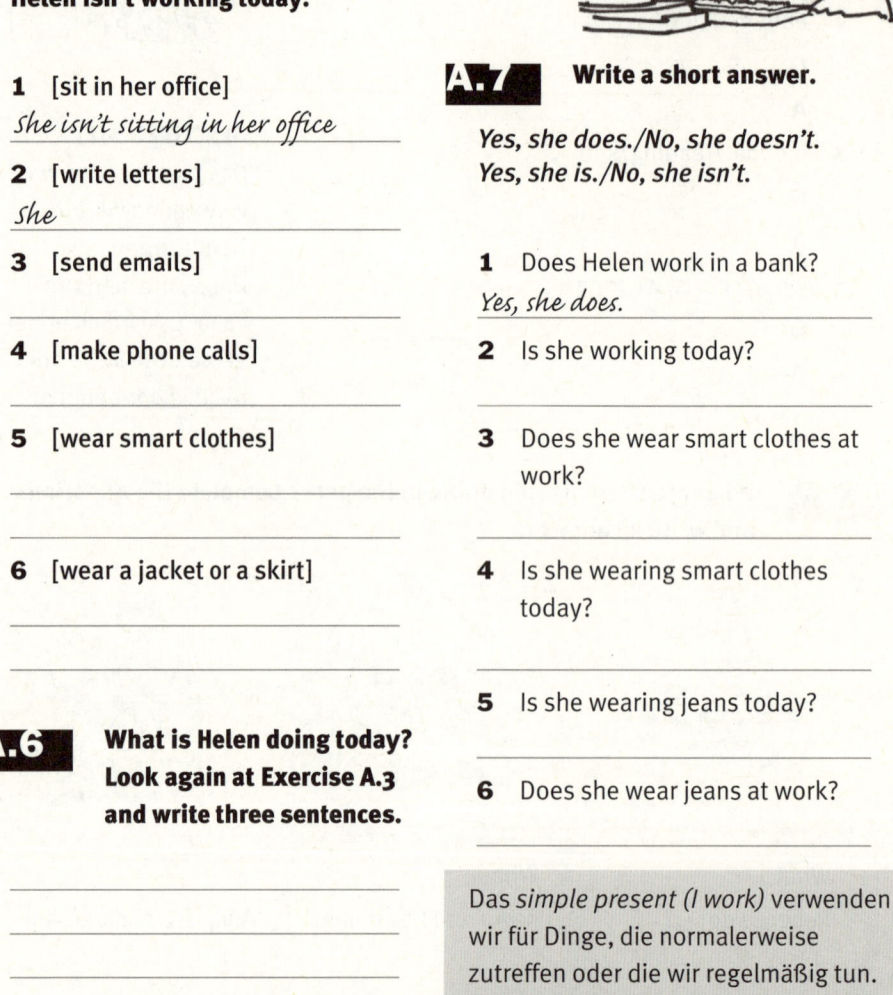

1 [sit in her office]
She isn't sitting in her office

2 [write letters]
She

3 [send emails]

4 [make phone calls]

5 [wear smart clothes]

6 [wear a jacket or a skirt]

A.6 What is Helen doing today? Look again at Exercise A.3 and write three sentences.

A.7 Write a short answer.

Yes, she does./No, she doesn't.
Yes, she is./No, she isn't.

1 Does Helen work in a bank?
Yes, she does.

2 Is she working today?

3 Does she wear smart clothes at work?

4 Is she wearing smart clothes today?

5 Is she wearing jeans today?

6 Does she wear jeans at work?

Das *simple present (I work)* verwenden wir für Dinge, die normalerweise zutreffen oder die wir regelmäßig tun. Das *present continuous (I'm working)* steht bei Dingen, die gerade im Moment bzw. im Zeitraum der unmittelbaren Gegenwart geschehen.

UNIT **8** Trends and sales **B** | 45

Reading

B.1 Read the text about Alpha Car Hire Ltd.

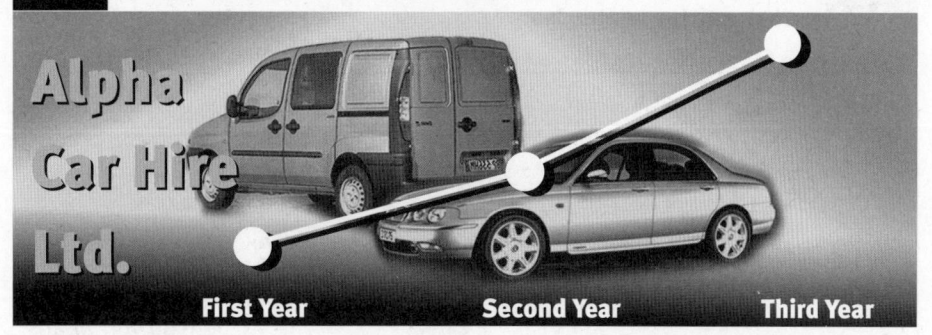

First Year   Second Year   Third Year

Alpha Car Hire Limited is based in Oxford, England. It is now three years old, and has 19 cars, 8 vans and 2 small lorries. In its first year, the company's turnover was about £200,000. Its volume of business grew in the second year, and rose again in the third.
Now in Alpha's fourth year, sales are up again and the company is planning two new offices: one at Heathrow Airport in London, and one in the north of England.

B.2 True or false? Write T or F.

1 Alpha Car Hire Ltd is an English company. _T_
2 Its head office is in Oxford. ___
3 Alpha's turnover in its first year was £1m. ___
4 Its sales grew in the second year. ___
5 They were down in its third year. ___
6 This year, sales are rising again. ___

VOCABULARY	
car	*Auto*
van	*Lieferwagen*
lorry	*LKW*
turnover	*Umsatz*
North of England	*Nordengland*

B.3 Answer the questions.

1 How many vans has Alpha Car Hire Ltd got now?

2 Did the company's sales rise or fall in its third year?

3 The company is now in its fourth year. Are its sales rising or falling at the moment?

4 Where is the company planning new offices?

EXTRA: Aussprache

B.4 Find the pairs of words *(Wortpaare)* that have the same sound. Then say the sentences.

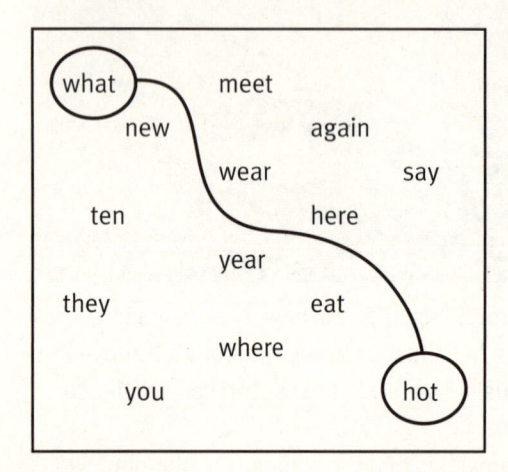

what — hot
meet
new
again
wear — say
ten
here
year
they
eat
where
you

What did they say?
When did you meet?
What did you eat?
Where do you wear your suit?
Are you new here?

Writing

B.5 Write about yourself. Write 40 – 60 words.

Where do you live? Do you work? What do you like doing? What are you doing at the moment? Where are you at the moment? What are you wearing?

9 Arrangements

Zeitausdrücke

A.1 Write in the prepositions.

1. _on_ Saturday
2. _____ half past nine
3. _____ Monday morning
4. _____ the afternoon
5. _____ the 23rd of June
6. _____ Tuesday
7. _____ 11 o'clock _____ the morning
8. _____ the 10th of May _____ midday

TIME EXPRESSIONS	
ON	Friday
	Tuesday morning
	the 10th of April
IN	the morning/ afternoon/evening
AT	11 o'clock/midday

Die Verlaufsform der Gegenwart mit Zukunftsbezug

A.2 Complete the text with verbs from the box.

Anita Robbins is a famous British businesswoman. She's the founder of the Body Company. It makes and sells natural cosmetic products. Anita has more than 150 Body Company shops in the UK and the USA. She's flying to the USA next week. She's opening a new Body Company shop in San Francisco. Here's her schedule.

's flying (x2)
's having
's opening
's visiting

Anita _'s flying_ to San Francisco on Monday morning. She _____¹ her new shop on Tuesday morning, then in the afternoon she _____² the Golden Gate Bridge. She _____³ dinner with the manager and staff of her new shop on Tuesday evening. Anita _____⁴ back to London on the 5th of May.

VISIT TO SAN FRANCISCO

MONDAY	3rd MAY
10.00	Flight to San Francisco

TUESDAY	4th MAY
09.30	Open new shop
14.00	Visit Golden Gate Bridge
19.00	Dinner with manager and staff of new shop

WEDNESDAY	5th MAY
15.00	Flight back to London

UNIT 9 Arrangements A

Fragen stellen: *When are you ...ing?*

A.3 Ask Anita questions about her visit.

1 When _are you flying to San Francisco?_
  I'm flying to San Francisco **on Monday.**

2 When _____
  _____
  I'm opening my new shop **on Tuesday.**

3 What _____
  _____
  I'm visiting **the Golden Gate Bridge** in the afternoon.

4 Where _____
  I'm having dinner **in a restaurant** on Tuesday evening.

5 When _____
  I'm flying back **on the 5th of May.**

Verneinung: *I'm not ...ing*

A.4 Write (and complete) the sentences.

1 You're flying to San Francisco on Tuesday, Anita.
  Is that right?

  No, I'm not flying to San Francisco on Tuesday.
  I'm flying to San Francisco on Monday.

2 You're opening the new shop on Friday.
  Is that right?

  _____
  _____ on Tuesday.

3 You're having dinner with the US president.
  Is that right?

  _____
  _____ with the manager and employees of my new shop.

> **WORTSTELLUNG**
> Beachten Sie, dass im Englischen in Sätzen wie dem folgenden Orts- vor Zeitangaben stehen:
> *I'm flying to San Francisco* [ORT] *on Monday* [ZEIT].
> **NICHT:** ~~*I'm flying on Monday to San Francisco.*~~

Einen Termin vereinbaren

A.5 Complete the telephone dialogue with phrases from the box.

> possible | Good evening | that's fine | How about
> I'm tied up all day | are you doing | I'm free

Anita Robbins is in San Francisco. It's Monday evening and she's at her hotel.

MARTY Good evening, Ms Robbins. I'm Marty Jackson from CNN Business News.
ANITA _____¹, Mr Jackson. How can I help you?
MARTY Is it _____² that we can have a short interview with you?
ANITA Yes, OK.
MARTY What _____³ tomorrow?
ANITA I'm afraid _____⁴ tomorrow, Mr Jackson.
       But _____⁵ on Wednesday morning.
MARTY _____⁶ 9 o'clock at your hotel?
ANITA Yes, _____⁷.
MARTY Thank you very much. I'll see you then.

Das *will*-Futur für Versprechen: *I'll see you then*

A.6 Find the best phrases from the box and write them in.

1 ○ Are you free next week, Mary?
   ● _____

2 ○ There's a letter on your desk, Mike.
   ● _____

3 ○ Mrs Evans is at the reception desk.
   ● _____

4 ○ Can you find me a nice hotel, Jane?
   ● _____

> Thanks for a good meeting, Tom. I'll see you again next week.

Das *will*-Futur (*I'll* = *I will*) verwenden wir, um Versprechen auszudrücken.

A Thanks.
   I'll read it now.
B Certainly.
   I'll look on the Internet.
C Thanks.
   I'll come down.
D I'll look in my diary.

Am Telefon

B.1 Read the telephone conversation and complete Alice's message.

ALICE Gardener and Simmons Management Consultants. Alice speaking. How may I help you?

MAN Good morning. Can I speak to Mr Gardener, please? This is Arthur Cox from British Plastics Ltd.

ALICE I'm sorry, Mr Cox, Mr Gardener isn't here today. Can I take a message?

MAN Yes, thank you. Can you say: 'thank you' for his report, and how about a meeting on Wednesday or Thursday next week?

ALICE Fine. I've got that.

MAN Thank you very much.

TELEPHONE MESSAGE

DATE: June 4
TIME: 12.45
FROM: _____
_____
_____
RE: _____
_____
_____
_____

B.2 Choose the best answer. Underline a, b or c.

1 Good morning.
   a Goodbye.
   b Good morning.
   c This is Simon speaking.

2 Can you spell your name, please?
   a It's 456 128.
   b C-H-R-I-S-T-I-E. Christie.
   c Thank you very much.

3 Who's calling, please?
   a Sales department.
   b I've got that. I'll tell Ann.
   c It's Kerstin Willers from Germany.

4 Thank you very much.
   a You're welcome.
   b Please.
   c Good morning.

5 Can I speak to Chris, please?
   a Can I take a message?
   b One moment, please.
   c I'm fine, thanks. And you?

EXTRA: Zeitformen

B.3 Write the verbs in brackets [...] in the correct tense: the simple present *(I go)*, the simple past *(I went)* or the present continuous *(I'm going)*.

Anita Robbins __is__ [be] the founder of the Body Company.
She _____ ¹ [live] in London.
The Body Company _____ ² [begin] in 1987.
At first, *(Am Anfang)* Anita _____ ³ [make] her cosmetics at home.
They _____ ⁴ [be] very popular, and in 1991 she
_____ ⁵ [open] her first shop. Now she _____ ⁶ [have]
over 150 shops, and next week she _____ ⁷ [open] another new
shop in San Francisco. Anita _____ ⁸ [be] also a writer *(Schriftstellerin)*.
Two years ago she _____ ⁹ [write] 'The Body Company Story'.
At the moment she _____ ¹⁰ [write] a second book about the
company. She _____ ¹¹ [be] a very busy person!

EXTRA: Worträtsel

B.4 Write in the English words and find the business phrase!

1 Büro
2 Montag
3 Brief
4 Flug
5 Zeitung
6 heute
7 gewöhnlich
8 Gewinn
9 Fabrik
10 Handy
11 Urlaub
12 Schreibtisch
13 wieder
14 fünfzig

PHRASE:

_____
_____!

10 Travelling on business

Komparativ: ... -er than/more ... than

A.1 Complete the table. Then write words from the table in the sentences.

adjective	comparative
old	_____
cold	_____
long	_____
big	bigger
hot	_____
friendly	_____
busy	_____
famous	_____
exciting	_____
expensive	_____
beautiful	_____
interesting	_____

1 Montreal is a big city, but London is __bigger than__ Montreal.
2 Montreal is exciting, but London is _____ _____ Montreal.
3 London isn't cold in the winter. Montreal is _____ _____ London.
4 Montreal is a busy city but London is _____ _____ Montreal.
5 The River Thames is long but the River Lawrence is _____ _____ the Thames.
6 Montreal isn't an expensive city. London is _____ _____ Montreal.
7 Montreal is famous, but London is _____ _____ Montreal.

UNIT 10 Travelling on business A

Superlativ: *the ... -est/the most ...*

A.2 Complete the table (see exercise A.1) and write words again in the sentences.

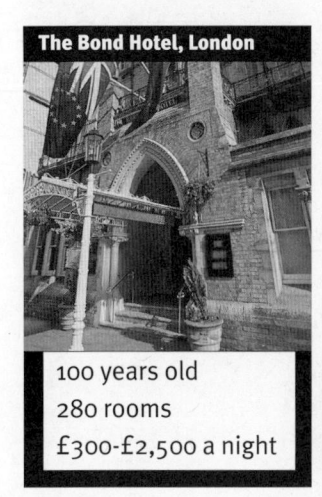

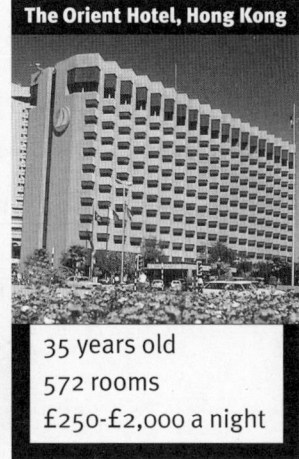

The Bond Hotel, London
100 years old
280 rooms
£300-£2,500 a night

The Orient Hotel, Hong Kong
35 years old
572 rooms
£250-£2,000 a night

The Rayad Hotel, Dubai
10 years old
811 rooms
£200-£850 a night

1 The Bond is 100 years old.
It's _the oldest_ hotel.

2 The Bond is £2,500 a night.
It's _____ hotel.

3 The Bond is very friendly, but _____ hotel is the Orient.

4 London and Dubai are busy cities, but Hong Kong is one of _____ _____ cities in the world.

superlative
the _oldest_
the _c_ 1
the _l_ 2
the _b_ 3
the _h_ 4
the _f_ 5
the _b_ 6
the _m f_ 7
the _m e_ 8
the _m e_ 9
the _m b_ 10
the _m i_ 11

A.3 Write answers for yourself.

1 The best day of the week is _____.
2 The best month of the year is _____.
3 The best movie in the last twelve months was _____.
4 The best newspaper for business is _____.

Which? (Welche/r/s?)

A.4 Look again at exercise A.2. Write the questions.

1 *Which is the most expensive hotel?*
   The Bond – it's £2,500 a night.

2 _____
   Also the Bond. It's 100 years old.

3 _____
   The Orient. The people there are very, very friendly.

4 _____
   Hong Kong. It's one of the busiest cities in the world.

Kreuzworträtsel

A.5 Complete the crossword. All the words are in Unit 10, Part A of your course book.

Down *(Senkrecht)*

1 Gast
2 Flughafen
3 ~ room = Einzelzimmer
5 Nächte
8 ~ room = Doppelzimmer
9 ~ 18 to 23 March
   = vom 18. bis 23. März

Across *(Waagerecht)*

4 ... date = Verfallsdatum
6 non-~ = Nichtraucher
7 ~ card = Kreditkarte
10 Besuch
11 Hotel

Im Hotel

B.1 Andrew Miller is arriving at a hotel. Complete his conversation with the receptionist.

*floor | stay | reserved
name's | newspaper
registration | fill | single
dining | key*

ANDREW Good afternoon. You've got a room _____¹ for me for this evening. My _____² Miller.

RECEPTIONIST Good afternoon, Mr Miller. Yes, a _____³ room with bath.

ANDREW That's right.

RECEPTIONIST Would you _____⁴ in the _____⁵ card, please? ... Here's your room _____⁶. It's room 24 on the first _____⁷. Breakfast is from six until half past nine in the _____⁸ room. Would you like a _____⁹ in the morning?

ANDREW Yes, *The Telegraph*, please.

RECEPTIONIST Certainly. Enjoy your _____¹⁰ with us, sir.

Writing

B.2 You are at the reception desk of the Golden Lion Hotel. Fill in the registration card for yourself.

```
            GOLDEN LION HOTEL
Surname:         Mr/Mrs/Ms/Dr _____
First Name(s):   _____
Nationality:     _____
Arrival Date     ___/___/___      Departure Date  ___/___/___
Car Registration
Number           _____

Payment:    Credit card [ ]    Cheque [ ]    Cash [ ]
```

Wegbeschreibungen

B.3 Look at the map and name the places.

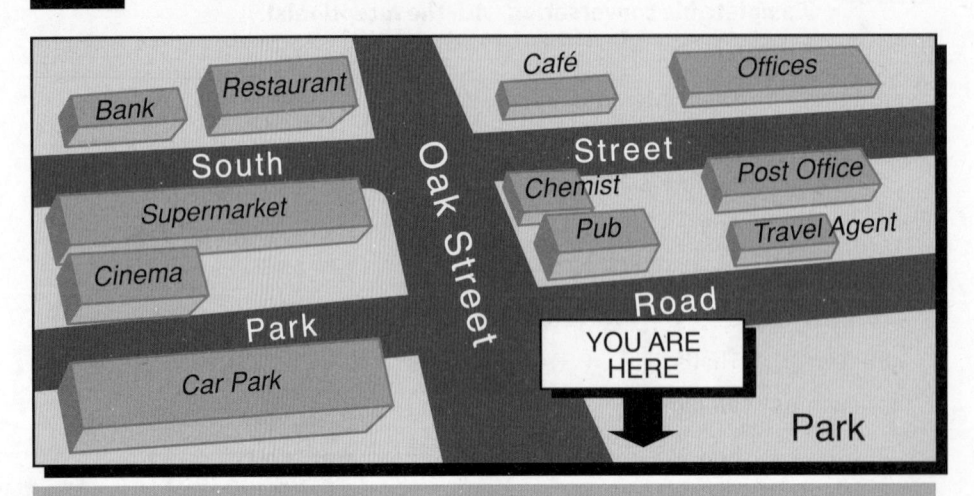

1. Go straight up Oak Street and take the first right. Go past the pub and the _travel agent_ is on the left.

2. Go straight up Oak Street and take the second left. Go past the restaurant and the _____ is on the right.

3. Go straight up Oak Street and take the second right. The _____ are on the left, opposite the post office.

4. Go straight up Oak Street and take the first left. The _____ is on the right, opposite the car park.

B.4 Write the directions.

1. Excuse me. How do I get to the post office, please?

2. Excuse me. Can you direct me to the supermarket, please?

Test 3

Check your English on units 8-10! *Kreuzen Sie die richtigen Antworten an. (Es gibt jeweils nur eine richtige Antwort.)*

	April
Monday **1st**	*interviews*
Tuesday **2nd**	*Flight to Toronto 2.00*
Wednesday **3rd**	*Flight back 07.30*
Thursday **4th**	*Presentation*
Friday **5th**	*Write report!*

This is Anne Lasselle.

This is her diary for next week.

Grammatik

1 Anne ... from Canada.
- a   come ☐
- b   comes ☐
- c   is coming ☐

2 She ... in Montreal.
- a   live ☐
- b   lives ☐
- c   is living ☐

3 At the moment, she ... at her desk.
- a   sit ☐
- b   sits ☐
- c   is sitting ☐

4 What ... next Monday?
- a   Anne is doing ☐
- b   is Anne doing ☐
- c   is doing Anne ☐

5 She's ...
- a   flying next Tuesday to Toronto. ☐
- b   flying to Toronto next Tuesday. ☐

6 On Friday she's ... a report.
- a   writeing ☐
- b   writing ☐
- c   writting ☐

Next month Anne Lasselle is going to London. Here are three hotels in London.

Park Royal Hotel ★★★★★

Somerset Lodge Hotel

Heathrow Inn

7 The ... hotel is the Heathrow Inn.
- a most big ☐
- b biggest ☐
- c most biggest ☐

8 The ... is the Park Royal.
- a most expensive ☐
- b expensivest ☐
- c most expensivest ☐

9 The Park Royal Hotel is ... the Somerset Lodge.
- a more expensive then ☐
- b expensiver than ☐
- c more expensive than ☐

10 ... hotel is the best of the three?
- a Where ☐
- b What ☐
- c Which ☐

Wortschatz

11 Next week I'm visiting one of my ... *(Kunden)* in London.
- a customers ☐
- b companies ☐
- c colleagues ☐

12 London is a very ... *(aufregend)* city.
- a pleasant ☐
- b exciting ☐
- c expensive ☐

13 I'm ... my visit. *(freue mich auf)*
- a looking at ☐
- b looking forward to ☐

14 Last year our sales ... *(wuchsen)* by 10%.
- a grew ☐
- b rose ☐
- c fell ☐

15 Sales this year are ... *(ausgezeichnet)* again.
- a excellent ☐
- b successful ☐
- c not so good ☐

16 ... they're up by 15%.
- a This far ☐
- b As far ☐
- c So far ☐

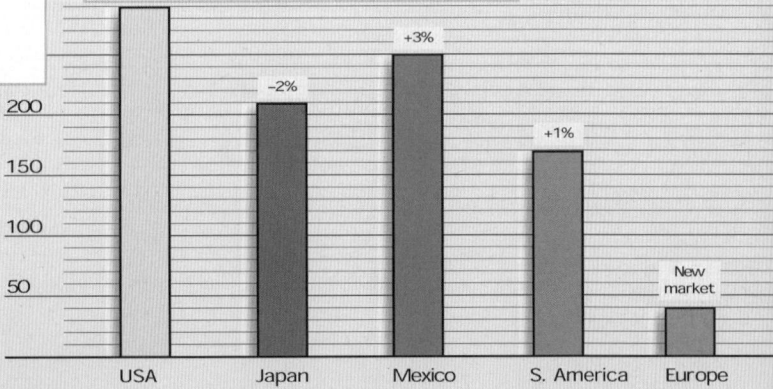

Situationen

Anne Lasselle is arriving at her hotel in London.

The receptionist is giving Anne directions to Luigi's.

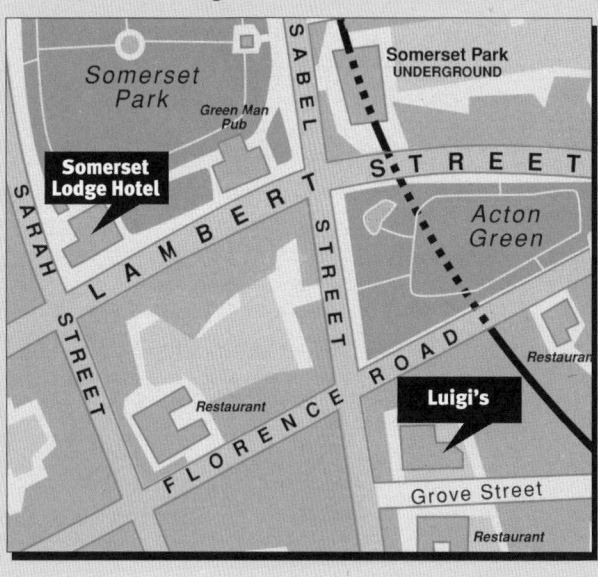

ANNE Good evening. You've got a room reserved for me.

RECEPTIONIST Yes, good evening, Ms Lasselle. A ... for two nights.

17
a one room ☐
b conference room ☐
c single room ☐

18 Would you fill in the ..., please?
a registration card ☐
b credit card ☐
c boarding card ☐

19 Here's your ... . It's room 211 on the second floor.
a cash ☐
b key ☐
c map ☐

20 Breakfast is from six until ten in the ... .
a fitness centre ☐
b lift ☐
c dining room ☐

21 Turn ... outside the hotel.
a left ☐
b right ☐

22 Go ... the Green Man pub.
a past ☐
b straight ☐

23 Turn right at the ... .
a lights traffic ☐
b traffic lights ☐

24 ... the second left.
a Go ☐
b Take ☐

25 Luigi's is ... the left.
a on ☐
b at ☐

Total   /25

Lösungen

UNIT 1 You and your job

Seite 4

A.1
1 'm   4 'm   7 're
2 'm   5 're
3 'm   6 're

A.2
1 She's   4 They're   7 It's
2 He's   5 They're
3 He's   6 It's

Seite 5

A.3
1 What's   3 you   5 from
2 are   4 Where

A.4
2 He's 28 (years old).
3 He's a sales manager.
4 They're tennis and swimming.
5 Where's Jill from?
6 How old is she?
7 What's her job?
8 What are her hobbies?

Seite 6

A.5
2 isn't   5 's
3 's   6 isn't
4 's   7 aren't, 're

A.6
1 My, your   3 Their   5 Our
2 Her   4 Its

A.7
FREIE ÜBUNG
Beispiel:
My name's …. I'm from … in ….
I'm a/an … (with a company in …).
My hobbies are ….

Seite 7

B.1
1 from   4 sorry   7 moment
2 speak   5 spell
3 please 6 Thank

B.2
1 Canada   4 Australia
2 South America 5 Japan
3 Africa   6 Asia

Seite 8

B.3
2 She's from Canada.
3 They're from Australia.

B.4
America	American
Asia	Asian
Australia	Australian
Britain	British
Canada	Canadian
Europe	European
Germany	German
Japan	Japanese

2 German   6 Canadian
3 African 7 European
4 Asian   8 British
5 American

UNIT 2 In the office

Seite 9

A.1
1 one   5 five   9 nine
2 two   6 six   10 ten
3 three   7 seven
4 four   8 eight

A.2
2 four lamps
3 ten telephones
4 nine photos
5 three faxes
6 eight secretaries
7 five diaries
8 six men
9 seven women
10 three people

A.3
2 He's got a plant.
3 He's got a diary.
4 He's got a telephone.
5 He's got a lamp.

Seite 10

A.4
2 I've got
3 I haven't got, I've got
4 I've got, I haven't got

A.5
2 Yes, she has.
3 No, she hasn't.
4 Yes, she has.
5 No, she hasn't.

A.6
2 has   4 has
3 is   5 is

Seite 11

A.7
2 False   5 True   8 False
3 True   6 True
4 False   7 False

A.8
1 There's a man behind the reception desk. (Satz 2)
2 There's one computer on the reception desk. (Satz 4)
3 There are two people near the lift. (Satz 7)
4 There's a telephone on the (reception) desk. Oder: There are two magazines on the table near the businessman. (Satz 8)

Seite 12

B.1
2 747 884   3 265 007   4 666 222

B.2
2 four five nine, three oh six two.
3 four five eight, double three one.
(US: four five eight, three three one)
4 double oh double four, two oh seven, three six five, double two one.
(US: oh oh four four two oh seven, three six five, two two one.)

B.3

1	is	8	call
2	from	9	Thank
3	please	10	number
4	afternoon	11	It's
5	sorry	12	313
6	office	13	Bye
7	Can		

Seite 13

B.4

- [s] desks, plants, restaurants
- [z] telephones, flowers, names, memos
- [iz] classes, bosses

B.5

1 DESK
2 THREE
3 PHOTOCOPIER
4 NEAR
5 CORNER
6 PRINTER
7 WALL
8 DOOR
9 DIARY

Lösungswort: **SECRETARY**

UNIT 3 People and companies

Seite 14

A.1

1	go: goes	3	speak: speaks
2	live: lives	4	work: works

A.2

2 lives
3 works
4 speaks, goes

Seite 15

A.3

1	lives	3	sells
2	makes	4	goes

A.4

1	comes	3	does, work, works
2	does, live	4	does, go, goes

A.5

1 She lives in Boston.
2 It makes clothing.
3 It sells its products worldwide.
4 She goes to Europe and Japan (every year).

Seite 16

A.6

1 comes
2 doesn't live, lives
3 speaks, doesn't speak

A.7

Korrekte Sätze:
2 a 3 b 4 a

Seite 17

B.1

1 a
2 sales representative
3 Bell
4 Danbury
5 Market
6 two oh one, double four seven
7 dot west at bell dot co dot uk

B.2

2 b 4 a 6 a
3 c 5 c

Seite 18

B.3

2 Joanne Taylor
3 Susan Harper
4 Pamela Baker
5 Susan Harper
6 Donald Winter

B.4

2 Harper's 4 manager's
3 Baker's

UNIT 4 Daily routines

Seite 19

A.1

1 start 3 eat 5 go
2 have   4 finish

A.2

	TO WORK	TO GO	TO HAVE
I	work	go	have
he/she/it	works	goes	has
we/you/they	work	go	have

Seite 20

A.3

2 does 5 do 8 do
3 does 6 do
4 does 7 do

A.4

1 doesn't 3 don't 5 doesn't
2 doesn't 4 don't

Seite 21

A.5

2 I normally go to work by car.
3 I often have lunch in the canteen.
4 I sometimes go to a café.
5 I'm always busy.
6 I'm never late.

A.6

1 eleven o'clock
2 half-past three
3 a quarter to five
4 a quarter past eight
5 twenty-five to seven
6 twenty-five past six
7 ten to nine
8 ten past nine
9 midday
10 midnight

Seite 22

B.1

1 watching a live sport
2 45%
3 going to theme parks.
4 like
5 66%, keeping fit

B.2

FREIE ÜBUNG

Seite 23

B.3

A	B	C
morning	address	company
jogging	canteen	popular
minutes		family
colleagues		
concerts		

B.4

FREIE ÜBUNG

Seiten 24, 25

TEST 1					
1	c	8	a	15	a
2	b	9	a	16	c
3	d	10	b	17	b
4	b	11	a	18	a
5	c	12	d	19	b
6	a	13	a	20	c
7	b	14	b		

UNIT 5 Doing business

Seite 26

A.1

1. THURSDAY
2. MONDAY
3. SATURDAY
4. TUESDAY
5. FRIDAY
6. SUNDAY
7. WEDNESDAY

Lösungswort: **ROUTINE**

A.2

2. was
3. had
4. was
5. was

Seite 27

A.3

I	was
he/she/it	was
we/you/they	were

2. was, was
3. were, were

A.4

1. b 2. c 3. b

A.5

2. the first of April
3. the second of March
4. the third of January
5. the tenth of September
6. the thirtieth of December
7. the twenty-first of June
8. the twenty-ninth of October

Seite 28

B.1

1. She's a secretary.
2. Shopping at the supermarket (was always a problem).
3. She visits it every Thursday evening.
4. She pays by credit card.
5. On Fridays at four o'clock.

Seite 29

B.2

Die folgenden Wörter sollten durchgestrichen werden:
2. where 4. no 6. our
3. there 5. go

B.3

2. Where 4. please
3. address 5. Their

UNIT 6 A visit to a company

Seite 30

A.1

2. travelled 4. talked, discussed
3. stayed

The Simple Past (regular verbs)			
	to visit	to travel	to arrive
I	visited	travelled	arrived
he/she/it	visited	travelled	arrived
we/you/they	visited	travelled	arrived

Seite 31

A.2

2. went 3. had 4. took

A.3

1. travelled   7. talked
2. flew   8. discussed
3. arrived   9. had
4. took   10. went
5. stayed   11. returned
6. went

Seite 32

A.4

2. How did she travel?
3. When did she fly?
4. When did she arrive?
5. How did she go to the airport?
6. Where did she stay?
7. When did she go to her client's office?
8. What did they talk about?
9. Where did they have lunch?
10. When did Jane return to London?

A.5

2. Jane didn't go to her hotel by limousine!
3. Jane didn't stay at the Schweizerhof Hotel!
4. Jane didn't have lunch with Steven Spielberg!

Seite 33

B.1

1. PA   5. a coffee
2. meet   6. could I
3. flight   7. along the corridor
4. Would you like

B.2

FREIE ÜBUNG

Seite 34

B.3

2. France   5. Spain
3. Switzerland   6. Holland
4. Greece   7. Iceland

B.4

Belgium	Belgian
Denmark	Danish
Finland	Finnish
France	French
Germany	German
(Great) Britain	British
Greece	Greek
Holland	Dutch
Iceland	Icelandic
Ireland	Irish
Italy	Italian
Luxembourg	Luxembourgian
Norway	Norwegian
Portugal	Portuguese
Spain	Spanish
Sweden	Swedish
Switzerland	Swiss

2. German   5. Dutch
3. Swiss   6. Italian
4. Irish   7. Swedish

UNIT 7 Facts and figures

Seite 35

A.1

1. company   6. based
2. began   7. president
3. sells   8. worldwide
4. shops   9. employees
5. customers 10. profit

A.2

1. the company's head office is in
2. the company was established
3. the company manufactures

Seite 36

A.3

2. How much coffee?   26 gallons
3. How much soda?   47 gallons
4. How many hamburgers?   150
5. How much ice-cream?   24 pounds
6. How many eggs?   243
7. How much cheese?   28 pounds
8. How much popcorn?   15 gallons

Seite 37

A.4
1. a lot of/many
2. a lot of
3. much
4. A lot of/many
5. many
6. a lot of
7. a lot of

A.5
2. one pound fifty
3. seven pounds fifty
4. two pounds ninety-nine
6. one/a dollar fifty
7. six dollars fifty/six dollars and fifty cents
8. twenty-three dollars ninety-nine/ and ninety-nine cents
10. three euros fifty/three euros and fifty cents
11. ten euros sixty five/and sixty-five cents
12. fifty cents

Seite 38

B.1
1. He invented corn flakes.
2. His brother, William Keith.
3. They opened their factory in 1906.
4. In 1909 they sold a million boxes of corn flakes per day.
5. Today Kellogg's sells its products in over 160 countries.

Seite 39

B.2

A	B	C
moment	discuss	conference
telephone	Japan	document
August		normally
product		president
student		secretary
total		

B.3

```
  F L E W
      E
      E
B E G A N   S
    O   T O O K
M E T       L
A       H A D
D I D   T
E       S E N T
```

Seite 40, 41

TEST 2

1 a	8 a	15 c
2 a	9 b	16 a
3 a	10 c	17 a
4 b	11 a	18 b
5 c	12 c	19 c
6 c	13 d	20 c
7 a	14 a	

UNIT 8 Trends and sales

Seite 42

A.1
2. He's drinking
3. he's making
4. He's reading
5. He's eating
6. He's writing

A.2
2. sending
3. working
4. speaking
5. smoking
6. wearing
7. saying
8. going
9. coming
10. jogging

Seite 43

A.3
2. What is Helen eating?
   She's eating an apple.
3. What is she reading?
   She's reading a book.
4. What is she wearing?
   She's wearing jeans and a T-shirt.

A.4
2. What are Kevin and Roy doing?
   They're playing football.
3. What are Ann, Lisa and Caroline doing?
   They're reading a magazine.

Seite 44

A.5
2. She isn't writing letters.
3. She isn't sending emails.
4. She isn't making phone calls.
5. She isn't wearing smart clothes.
6. She isn't wearing a jacket or a skirt.

A.6
Helen is sitting in the park. She's eating an apple and reading a book. She's wearing jeans and a T-shirt.

A.7
2. No, she isn't.
3. Yes, she does.
4. No, she isn't.
5. Yes, she is.
6. No, she doesn't.

Seite 45

B.1
FREIE ÜBUNG

B.2
2 T 4 T 6 T
3 F 5 F

B.3
1. Alpha Car Hire has got eight vans./ They've got eight vans.
2. They rose in its third year.
3. Sales are rising at the moment.
4. It's/they're planning new offices at Heathrow Airport in London and in the north of England.

Seite 46

B.4

what	hot
meet	eat
new	you
again	ten
wear	where
say	they
here	year

B.5
FREIE ÜBUNG

UNIT 9 Time expressions

Seite 47

A.1
2. at
3. on
4. in
5. on
6. on
7. at, in
8. on, at

A.2
1. 's opening
2. 's visiting
3. 's having
4. 's flying

Seite 48

A.3
2. When are you opening your new shop?
3. What are you doing in the afternoon?
4. Where are you having dinner on Tuesday evening?
5. When are you flying back?

A.4

2 No, I'm not opening the new shop on Monday. I'm opening it ...
3 No, I'm not having dinner with President Bush. I'm having dinner ...

Seite 49

A.5

1 Good evening
2 possible
3 are you doing
4 I'm tied up all day
5 I'm free
6 How about
7 that's fine

A.6

1 I'll look in my diary.
2 Thanks. I'll read it now.
3 Thanks. I'll come down.
4 Certainly. I'll look on the Internet.

Seite 50

B.1

From: Arthur Cox from British Plastics Ltd.
Re: Says thank you for his report. How about a meeting on Wednesday or Thursday next week?

B.2

1 b   3 c   5 b
2 b   4 a

Seite 51

B.3

1 lives   7 is opening
2 began   8 is
3 made   9 wrote
4 were   10 is writing
5 opened   11 is
6 has

B.4

OFFICE
MONDAY
LETTER
FLIGHT
NEWSPAPER
TODAY
USUALLY
PROFIT
FACTORY
MOBILE
HOLIDAY
DESK
AGAIN
FIFTY

Phrase: **I'm tied up all day!**

UNIT 10 Travelling on business

Seite 52

A.1

adjectives	comparatives
old	older
cold	colder
long	longer
big	bigger
hot	hotter
friendly	friendlier
busy	busier
famous	more famous
exciting	more exciting
expensive	more expensive
beautiful	more beautiful
interesting	more interesting

2 more exciting than
3 colder than
4 busier than
5 longer than
6 more expensive than
7 more famous than

Seite 53

A.2

superlative
1 the coldest
2 the longest
3 the biggest
4 the hottest
5 the friendliest
6 the busiest
7 the most famous
8 the most exciting
9 the most expensive
10 the most beautiful
11 the most interesting

2 the most expensive
3 the friendliest
4 the busiest

A.3

FREIE ÜBUNG

Seite 54

A.4

2 Which is the oldest hotel?
3 Which is the friendliest hotel?
4 Which is the busiest city, London, Dubai or Hong Kong?

A.5

GUEST / AIRY / EXPIRY / SINGLE / SMOKING / CREDIT / FROM / HOTEL / VISIT (crossword)

Seite 55

B.1

1 reserved   6 key
2 name's   7 floor
3 single   8 dining
4 fill   9 newspaper
5 registration 10 stay

B.2

1 FREIE ÜBUNG

Seite 56

B.3

2 bank   3 offices   4 cinema

B.4

VORSCHLÄGE
1 Go straight up Oak Street and take the second right. Go past the chemist and the post office is on the right.
2 Go straight up Oak Street and take the second left. The supermarket is on the left, opposite the restaurant (and the bank).

Seiten 57-59

TEST 3

1 b	10 c	19 b
2 b	11 a	20 c
3 c	12 b	21 a
4 b	13 b	22 a
5 b	14 a	23 b
6 b	15 a	24 b
7 b	16 c	25 a
8 a	17 c	
9 c	18 a	